Roll on, thou deep
and dark blue Ocean — roll!
Ten thousand fleets
sweep over thee in vain;
Man marks the earth with ruin —
his control
Stops with the shore.

Lord Byron
from *Childe Harold's Pilgrimage*

Copyright © 1993 Space Biospheres Ventures. All rights reserved.
Library of Congress Catalog Card no. 93-072820. ISBN 1-882428-02-1.
Printed in Mexico on recycled and recyclable paper.

INSIDE
BIOSPHERE 2

The Ocean
and
Its Reef

Linnea Gentry

THE BIOSPHERE PRESS / Oracle, Arizona

MORPHO
BUTTERFLY

ROOSTER

THE BREATHTAKING STRUCTURE OF BIOSPHERE 2

STEELHEAD TROUT

I n the southwestern corner of the United States on the slopes

of a desert mountain range, an unusual glass greenhouse stretches

over an area the size of three football fields. Inside this huge

glass and steel structure are miniature replicas

of five separate tropical habitats:

a rainforest, a savannah, a desert,

a marsh, and an ocean.

DOLIUM SHELL

Modeled after these regions as they naturally

exist on Earth, these five wilderness zones and

their plant, animal, and microscopic inhabitants are

completely sealed off from the foundation of Earth below

them and the atmosphere of Earth above them. They are

BAMBOO

BULLFROG

SPRAWLS BENEATH THE ARIZONA SUN.

ORANGE TREE FLOWER

GALAGO

being cared for and studied by a crew of men and women who live inside this fascinating world — also sealed off from the outside. They raise their own food and recycle everything within their walls. Nothing but sunlight, sound, electricity, and scientific samples pass through the glass panes or airlock hatches. Its builders call this experiment Biosphere 2 since it is the offspring of the only other biosphere we know — Earth (sometimes called Biosphere 1).

THE FIRST CREW TO
LIVE IN BIOSPHERE 2

LEAF BEETLE

HUMMINGBIRD

SOFT-SHELLED
TURTLE

It is a unique world, full of its own beauty and mystery. Shady paths twist through bowers of green branches. One stream splashes down the face of a miniature mountain. Another winds in wide loops through the grasses of a savannah. Animals rustle under the cover of dry leaves, and palm branches sway over a tiny sandy beach.

The people who built this world are studying it to find out more about how our planet works. In creating a miniature model of Earth that can be closely watched and analyzed, they hope to learn some of the secrets of the balance of forces that have made our world what it is.

Some of those secrets can be discovered in that marvel of our planet, the ocean.

A SCHOOL OF ANCHOVIES SWIMS BY A REEF. ➤

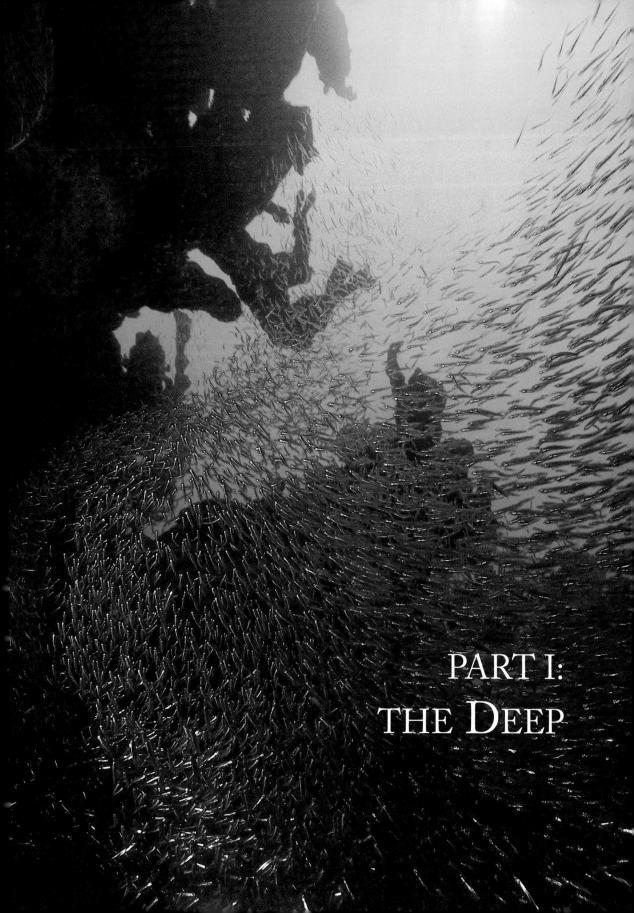

PART I:
THE DEEP

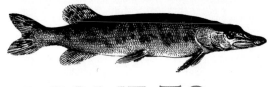

WELCOME TO PLANET OCEAN

From far out in space, Earth looks much like any other satellite reflecting back our sun's cold white light. But if visitors from Outer Space were to come in for a closer look — say, within half a million miles — they would soon notice the blue and white patterns swirling and drifting all around the planet. And if those visitors had the right equipment on their spaceship, they would easily recognize the presence of water in great abundance. From space, the fascinating interaction of Earth's water and its atmosphere can be seen in constant motion.

In fact, over 70% of the Earth's surface is water, a huge hydrosphere that exists in many forms — rivers, lakes, rain, ice, glaciers.

But to most of us who live here on Earth and to the visitors from Outer Space, the largest and most obvious mass of water is the ocean.

Huge, mysterious, and ever changing yet ever the same, it covers Earth so generously that you might well wonder why our planet wasn't named 'Ocean'.

Hydrosphere:
All the water on the Earth's surface, including the moisture in the atmosphere.

EARTH AS SEEN FROM THE SPACE SHUTTLE

Although the entire ocean is interconnected, it is divided into the Atlantic, Pacific, Indian, and Arctic Oceans by the six continents. Some people consider the Antarctic area of water a separate ocean, but it is completely open to the Atlantic, Pacific, and Indian Oceans with no land masses between.

Smaller areas of these four main oceans are called seas, as in the Mediterranean Sea or the Caribbean Sea. Before people knew the full extent of our ocean, it was called the Seven Seas more often than anything else.

It has also been called by other names: the Great Deep, the Bounding Main, the Abyss. In many languages its name is related to the word for mother, as in 'la mer' in French. But whatever our native language, for all of us the sea was the cradle of life.

It was in the watery deep of the ocean that life on Earth first began. Some scientists suggest that living organisms first appeared at 'hot springs' coming out of the Earth's crust deep down on the ocean floor. But, as often happens in science, we will probably never know for sure. We do know that all living organisms — bacteria, plants, animals, and others — gradually evolved for some three billion years in the ocean before moving onto dry land.

For a long time scientists thought that the ocean was created over millions of years as volcanic activity within and on the planet released drops of water and water vapor that gradually drained down the higher slopes of crust into the oceanic basins. More recent findings have revealed that water may also have come up out of the cracks in the Mid-Atlantic Rift at the time the seafloor crust was forming. Scientists have dubbed this form of new seawater 'juvenile water'.

Although it was once home to all living things, we do not know the ocean very well. It is really only the thin top layer, its outer surface, that we humans are most familiar with. People have been living along its shores and skimming across its surface for many thousands of years. But it is only in the past hundred and fifty years or so that we have begun to study it in earnest, to investigate its many secrets, to learn all that it is and does.

We do know that the ocean is a crucial part of the way the Earth system works and is vital to the support of life on our planet, even the life on land. It is the foundation of the entire hydrosphere, containing 97% of all the water on the planet. The remaining water of the hydrosphere is in rivers, lakes, clouds, and — especially — in the ice of the polar ice caps.

Sometimes when you look out to sea from the shore, it is hard to tell where the ocean ends and the sky begins. Although that's an optical illusion from your point of view — for of course, you can always tell when you're in water or out of it — from an atmospheric point of view, the distinction is sometimes difficult to make. The atmosphere and hydrosphere are constantly interacting together. We usually can't see those interactions very clearly, but sometimes, in the form of hurricanes for example, we can see the joining of ocean and atmosphere all too well.

Almost anywhere on Earth, the daily weather forecasts on radio and television usually include the origin of a particular storm or weather system over a large body of seawater, usually long before the storm appears overhead and dumps rain or snow on our own roofs. It's a complex process: air keeping water moving, water keeping air moving, and all of this prompted by the movement of the planet as it rotates on its axis.

The fascinating mix of hydrosphere and atmosphere is a primary force that helps to keep our basic planetary elements in

FISHERMENS' DORIES

FULL-SAILED FRIGATE

ROMAN TRIREME

OUTRIGGER CANOE

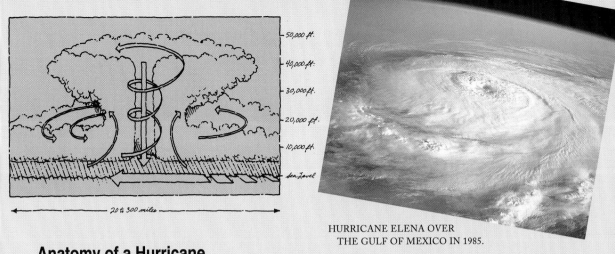

HURRICANE ELENA OVER
THE GULF OF MEXICO IN 1985.

Anatomy of a Hurricane

Scientists are still not sure exactly how the great storms, called hurricanes in the Atlantic, typhoons in the Pacific, and tropical cyclones in the Indian Ocean, come into being. These incredibly powerful weather systems form in ocean areas where warm air loses pressure, or 'thins out' — so much that the air on the surface of the water begins to spin inward and form a rotating circle of air. The circle of air usually measures about 20 miles across. This spinning swirl picks up moisture from the ocean and pushes it up tens of thousands of feet (sometimes as much as ten miles) above the surface. There it cools and forms rain, which is then pushed outward with terrific force. As this spiraling column of air and water moves across the ocean, it picks up speed.

A tropical storm is not a hurricane, typhoon, or tropical cyclone until it reaches winds of 75 miles per hour or more. Some hurricane wind speeds have been clocked at as much as 160 miles per hour! And some storms have reached diameters of as much as 300 miles across between the tips of their spirals.

Hurricanes and typhoons move westward at about ten miles per hour during their early stages before they turn towards the Poles. (North Atlantic hurricanes turn to the North Pole, South Atlantic hurricanes turn towards the South Pole. Typhoons and tropical cyclones do likewise.) These huge moving columns of atmospheric contortion may last anywhere from 1 to 30 days and can do terrible damage to coastlines, ships, people, buildings, crops, and wildlife.

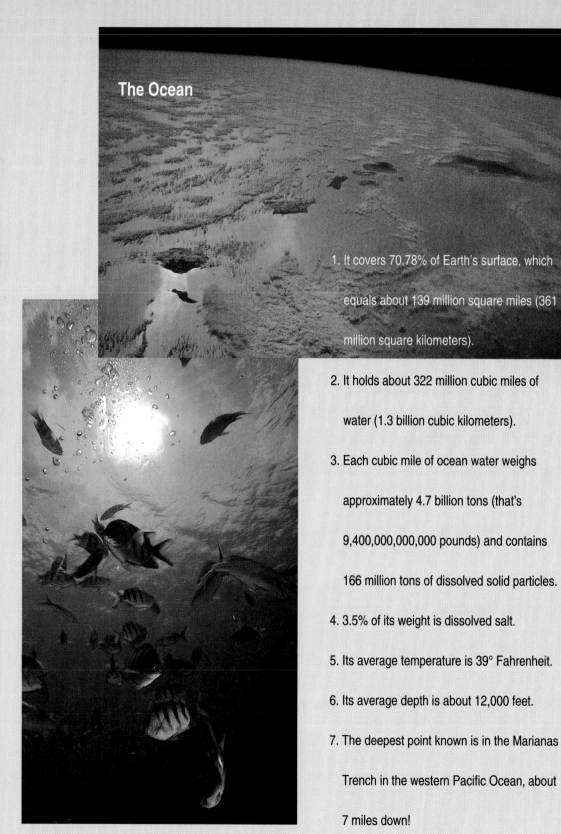

The Ocean

1. It covers 70.78% of Earth's surface, which equals about 139 million square miles (361 million square kilometers).

2. It holds about 322 million cubic miles of water (1.3 billion cubic kilometers).

3. Each cubic mile of ocean water weighs approximately 4.7 billion tons (that's 9,400,000,000,000 pounds) and contains 166 million tons of dissolved solid particles.

4. 3.5% of its weight is dissolved salt.

5. Its average temperature is 39° Fahrenheit.

6. Its average depth is about 12,000 feet.

7. The deepest point known is in the Marianas Trench in the western Pacific Ocean, about 7 miles down!

constant motion. Those elements are in many forms — some as liquids, some as gases, some as solid particles in rock or soil, and some in the cell structures of living and dead organisms. The interaction helps keep the basic elements as well as other things moving, such as the different water currents in the ocean.

The rhythms of the ocean are complicated even more by the tides, the alternating rise and fall of sea level caused by the pull of the sun and moon. The pull of these celestial bodies on our planet (or any other body) is part of the force of gravitation. Because the moon is so much closer to Earth than the sun, it exerts the greatest force in creating tides. At any given time, there are two rises of sea level, or high tides, on Earth. One is on the side facing the moon; the other, strangely enough, is on the opposite side. Tides in the main body of the ocean are usually fairly regular — high tides occurring about every 12½ hours. Tides in shallow areas, estuaries, or channels don't always follow this pattern. That's one reason why tide charts are so important to ships that are anywhere near land.

Despite the fact that the ocean is always in motion, it remains a force for stability in our system. It is especially important in keeping Earth's temperature relatively steady. The ocean cools or heats much more slowly than land and also holds heat much longer than the atmosphere does. So air passing over

According to a fanciful legend, the ancient Greek philosopher and naturalist Aristotle (AIR-es-TOT-uhl) flung himself into the sea and drowned because he was upset that he couldn't figure out how the tides worked. He shouldn't have taken the puzzle of tides so much to heart; they are a very complicated phenomenon.

water tends to pick up the water's temperature, rather than the other way around. In general, the warmer water flows toward the North and South Poles in the surface currents. The cold currents flow toward the Equator in the deeper ocean levels, which then warm up and rise in the equatorial belt.

Some of the atmosphere's energy comes from the processes related to the evaporation of seawater. But scientists do not yet clearly understand all the complex ways in which the ocean influences the atmosphere.

THE HAWAIIAN ISLANDS ARE DWARFED BY THE VAST PACIFIC OCEAN.

A SCHOOL OF SERGEANT MAJOR FISH

GOING DOWN

Under the waves is a whole different world — alien in many ways to us land creatures, yet always alluring. In the many layers and currents of ocean waters there lives an array of life forms just as amazing as any on land. And sometimes even more so! From the multitudes of zooplankton (zoe-PLANK-ten), the microscopic animals that float freely near the surface, to the giant sperm whales that can dive down as deep as a mile, to the strange fishes of the abyss that produce their own light — the ocean realm hosts the greatest diversity of life on the planet.

This abundance of life in different areas of the ocean is caused mostly by the available nourishment. The many zooplankton and tiny fishes which feed off the phytoplankton (FI-toe-PLANK-ten, tiny floating plants) form the base of nutrition for the ocean food web. These basic lifeforms are adapted to the temperatures and sunlight in their particular regions and currents.
The animals that prey on them in turn become prey for larger sea dwellers and form a web of interaction on 'up' to the top predators.

All of the lifeforms in the ocean's many parts make up a huge, interrelated living ecosystem.
Great schools of herring and squid, for example, travel the currents that crisscross the North Atlantic, eating the rich supplies of zooplankton in the cool northern waters. These relatively small schooling swimmers are eaten by the larger fish such as tuna, who in turn are eaten by even larger predators such as marlin and sharks.

Strangely enough, some of the largest animals in the food web, such as the basking sharks and the baleen whales, also live off plankton. The richest area of phytoplankton in the world appears in the summer in the Southern Hemisphere where warm currents coming down from the Equator meet the cold waters flowing away from Antarctica. The microscopic phytoplankton grow in these mixing currents and support vast populations of tiny, shrimplike krill. During the sunny months, eight species of whales, numerous seals, forty species of birds (from penguins to albatrosses), and millions of fish eat their fill of this protein-rich soup.

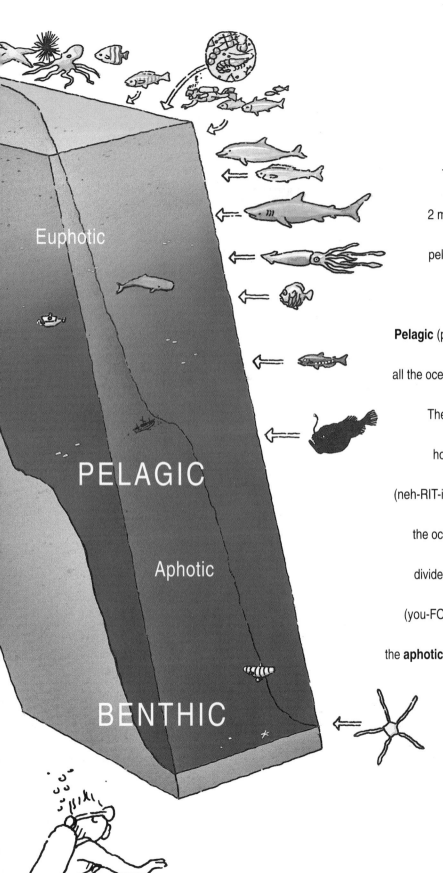

A Vertical Slice of the Ocean

The ocean is divided into 2 major realms: benthic and pelagic. **Benthic** (BEN-thic) refers to the ocean floor. **Pelagic** (peh-LADGE-ick) refers to all the ocean water above the floor. The pelagic realm is divided horizontally into the **neritic** (neh-RIT-ick, near-shore) area and the oceanic area. Vertically it is divided into the **euphotic** zone (you-FOE-tick, with sunlight) and the **aphotic** zone (A-foe-tick, without sunlight). The different lifeforms are adapted to these different zones.

Euphotic

PELAGIC

Aphotic

BENTHIC

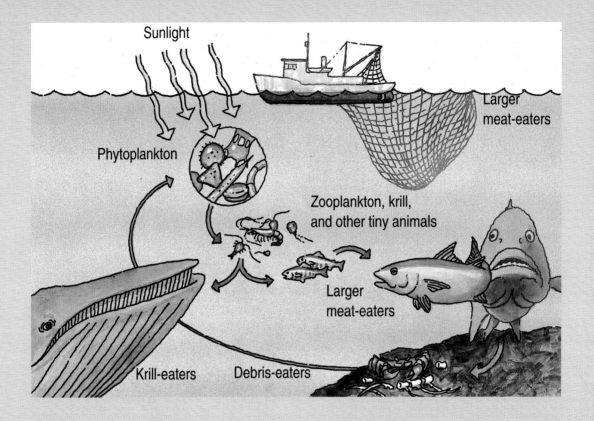

Sunlight

Phytoplankton

Zooplankton, krill,
and other tiny animals

Larger
meat-eaters

Larger
meat-eaters

Krill-eaters

Debris-eaters

An Ocean Food Web

Humans are a part of the ocean food web, too, although they are sometimes unaware that their hamburger may be part of the marine system. Many of the fish caught by fishing trawlers in the North Atlantic or North Pacific are added to food consumed by many of the cows and chickens that eventually wind up in fast-food outlets all across the United States. In fact, by 1980, 30% of the entire world's catch of fish went into livestock food and agricultural fertilizers! And that amount has continued to climb. In 1986 92.4 million tons (84 million metric tons) of fish were harvested from the ocean. Sadly, in the past twenty years the number of fish *available* as a world food resource, whether for us or for our livestock, has declined rapidly due to this unchecked overfishing.

Oceanographers and marine biologists are now working with fishing nations all over the world to better understand fish populations and to maintain a balanced, ecologically sound supply of different seafoods.

An interesting footnote in the story of life in the ocean is that of the coelacanth (SEE-lah-kanth), one of biology's strangest tales. The coelacanth was once known only by its fossil remains. It roamed the seas in great numbers in the Devonian Period of Earth's distant past some 400 million years ago. Its heavy, stout body and stumpy fins eventually evolved into the bodies and limbs of the amphibians. Everyone considered this animal extinct — until a fisherman caught a living specimen in the deep waters off South Africa. Since then, several more coelacanths, commonly called lobefins, have been caught in deep waters and studied.

The whales, fishes, and penguins who eat krill and the coelacanths in the deep are not the only stars of our huge oceanic system. Away from the polar regions, in the tropical and subtropical waters near the Equator, are some of the most dazzling and fascinating ecosystems on the planet, marine or terrestrial — the coral reefs.

Text continues on page 22

COELACANTH

SQUID

Suddenly we found ourselves transported into full light. I thought at first, of course, that the beacon [of the *Nautilus*] had been lighted and was again casting its electric radiance into the water. I was mistaken and, after a rapid survey, perceived my error. The *Nautilus* was floating in the midst of a phosphorescent mass which, because of the gloom elsewhere prevalent, became quite dazzling. The bright glow was produced by myriads of luminous animalculae, whose brilliancy was somehow increased as they glided over the hull of the vessel. I was amazed to see a sort of lightning in the center of these luminous sheets, as if rivulets of lead had been melted in a fiery furnace or metallic masses had been brought to a white heat . . . . Ah, no — this was not the ordinary irradiation of summer lightning. This was unusual burning and vigor, this was truly living light!

Professor Arronax describes an underwater scene while on board Captain Nemo's submarine, in one of the most famous sea adventures ever written, 20,000 Leagues Under the Sea *by Jules Verne (1870).*

The Art of Diving

THE *TRIESTE II* IN BOSTON HARBOR

Although our remote ancestors came out of the ocean, we humans can return to our ancestral home only if we take our atmosphere with us. Lack of oxygen and the increasing pressure of the water as it deepens have restricted our explorations for centuries. Yet men and women have always taken the risks and gone beneath the surface. Divers of the ancient world would hold their breath and dive for pearls as deep as 100 feet down in the Mediterranean. Divers in the waters of the Pacific still do it today.

In the seventeenth and eighteenth centuries, people got down to some serious engineering to solve the problems and developed the diving bell. This was an open-bottomed, bell-shaped chamber with a platform to stand on beneath it or with a seat attached inside it. As the diver in the bell was lowered into the water, the air became trapped and compressed in the top of the cone by the force of the water trying to rise. The diver could stay down for as long as the oxygen lasted but could only swim a short distance away, returning frequently for a new breath of air from the bell.

This restriction was overcome in the nineteenth century by the diving suit, made of a canvas body and a metal helmet with a tube supplying the diver with pressurized air from the surface. The diver could walk on the seafloor at whatever distance the tube would allow. Diving suits are still sometimes used today for special tasks, especially in shipbuilding and repair.

A SUBMARINE AS IMAGINED IN THE NINETEENTH CENTURY

The big step came when the French navy divers Emile Gagnan and Jacques-Yves Cousteau invented the aqualung during World War II. Now it is better known in the United States as SCUBA gear, SCUBA standing for self-contained underwater breathing apparatus. Divers could now go down about 200 feet and stay submerged for up to 2 hours. Not only did this invention revolutionize underwater military and salvaging operations, it generated a whole new era in recreation, tourism, and underwater archaeology. And now SCUBA gear is a very important tool in monitoring the ocean in Biosphere 2.

The development of submarine ships, or submersibles, have been just as enthusiastically pursued as personal diving equipment. Again, the invention and improvement of submarines were prompted by military motives: ships traveling virtually unseen under the waves were a tremendous advantage in war. In fact, the very first submarine was built by an American during the Revolutionary War to attack

THE DEEP SUBMERGENCE VEHICLE, *TURTLE*

British ships. It wasn't until the twentieth century that submarines were used more successfully. Most were developed for military purposes; but in the 1930s naturalist William Beebe and engineer Otis Barton created a steel diving capsule in which divers could study the marine world as deep as 3,000 feet down. Improvements are always being made. Now many types of submersibles, both manned and unmanned, explore our seas. Some look for oil, natural gas, and mineral deposits. Some search for ship wrecks to retrieve sunken treasures or to excavate for archaeological and historical purposes. And some are used for scientific research of all kinds.

One of the most famous submersibles is probably the U.S. Navy's *Alvin*. *Alvin* successfully carried explorer Robert Ballard and crew down to the bottom of the North Atlantic to the once-magnificent ocean liner *Titanic,* lying in its 74-year-old grave under almost 14,000 feet of icy water. The French submersible *Trieste* has made the deepest dive, over 36,000 feet to the bottom of the Pacific.

NINETEENTH-CENTURY DIVING BELL

RAINFOREST OF THE SEAS

Coral reefs are one of Earth's most delightful attractions. But those visitors from Outer Space circling the planet in a spaceship several miles up would probably miss them. Coral reefs grow under water, only occasionally showing above the surface during low tides. If the visitors were to put on snorkels or SCUBA tanks and masks and go under the waves, they would discover a world of breathtaking diversity and beauty. For a coral reef is a complete community of microscopic organisms, plants, and animals, comparable to the colorful variety and complexity of life in a tropical rainforest on land.

As in a rainforest, the sunlight filters down through the layers of water. Each layer supports particular plants and animals. The slopes of a healthy coral reef are a natural garden of many types of corals of different colors, shapes, and sizes. Lavender-colored staghorn coral may reach up into the currents above green brain corals and softly waving orange sea fans. A colorful array of fish, snails, jellyfish, anemones, brittlestars, crabs, and numerous other sea dwellers, also in all shapes and sizes, lives on and around the coral reefs.

People have given these lifeforms some wonderful names: lettuce-leaf coral, pillow stinking sponge, donkey dung sea cucumber, stoplight parrotfish, deadman's fingers, lemon-peel angelfish, chicken liver sponge, flamingo tongue snail, ass's ear abalone, bubble coral, crown-of-thorns starfish, ghost pipefish, moon jelly, flaming shamefaced crab — to mention just a few! All of these strange-sounding creatures have learned to live in a community of harmonious interaction that encourages the survival of hundreds of different **species** (SPEE-sheeze). Like any community, it's made up of a combination of inhabitants and events. But what makes all this jumble of life happen? What's at the bottom of it?

Species: A group of living individuals with similar characteristics which can breed with each other.

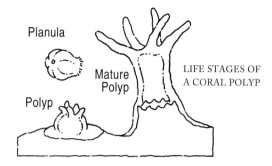

Planula

Mature Polyp

Polyp

Basically, it's all because of a little marine animal called the **polyp** (POL-ip). The polyp has a soft body, usually less than a half inch long, and protects itself by creating its own hard skeleton outside its body. Coral polyps hatch from eggs and often float away from their home colony. Sometimes they drift on currents for miles before they sink down and attach themselves to a hard, flat surface where the seawater, temperature, and sunlight are right for growth.

Once a reef-building coral polyp has found a suitable resting place, it will begin to create its exterior skeleton with the help of a special **algae** (AL-gee) called **zooxanthellae** (zoe-zann-THEL-lie). These tiny, one-celled plant algae

live inside the polyp's body, feeding on the available sunlight and the polyp's waste products while enjoying a comfortable, safe habitat. But the important thing, as far as coral reefs are concerned, is what the coral polyp gets in return. With the algae's help, the polyp is able to convert the **calcium salts** in the seawater into the 'limestone' (or, **calcium carbonate**) skeleton in which it lives. It's a relationship developed for the mutual benefit of both parties — a **symbiosis** (sim-by-O-sis).

From then on, the coral polyp lives out its watery life rooted to that one spot. It emerges from its skeleton (usually at night) to catch and eat tiny floating plankton with the ring of tentacles around its mouth. (Like other **invertebrates**, it doesn't have a face such as mammals, reptiles, or fish do.) During the day, it retreats into the safety of its limestone home.

The hill-like structure of the reef forms over a period of many, many years as coral polyps die and leave their empty skeletons behind. Generation after generation, new coral polyps emerge as buds from the parent polyps and attach themselves to the rising collection of calcium carbonate

A YELLOWTAIL SNAPPER AND A SERGEANT MAJOR SWIM BY OUTCROPPINGS OF LEAF LETTUCE CORAL AND BOULDER CORAL.

There are three different types of coral reef. **Atolls** (eh-TOLs) are reefs in the shape of a ring, rather like a doughnut, surrounded by the foaming breakers on the outside but encircling calm expanses of water within, called **lagoons** (lah-GOONS). These atolls often support tropical islands with beautiful sandy beaches, palm trees, and wildlife above the coral reef hidden under the waves.

Barrier reefs are long, narrow formations separated from the land by an equally long channel of calm seawater. Usually a white line of breakers crashes rhythmically against the seaward side of the reef, with here and there a little islet appearing above the water. The Great Barrier Reef off the coast of Australia is a series of barrier reefs loosely linked together.

Fringing reefs lie in shallow water closer to shore than barrier reefs. They're smaller and don't have the broad channel of deep water between themselves and the coastline. Many of the islands in the Caribbean Sea south of the United States are surrounded by fringing reefs. If you know how to swim and have a snorkel, mask, and fins, they are easy and fun to visit!

skeletons in larger and larger colonies of thousands — sometimes even millions — of polyps. Sometimes these colonies create series of reefs hundreds of miles long. The Great Barrier Reef, off the east coast of Australia, has taken 8 million years to grow to its current size of 1400 miles long. It takes years to explore that one!

THE ISLAND OF BOLABOLA AND ITS FRINGING REEF SKETCHED BY CHARLES DARWIN

Not only does the algae give the polyp its protective skeleton, but the collection of skeletons rising up toward the sunlight provides hundreds of other creatures with a habitat in which to grow and reproduce. Manatee and turtle grasses, other forms of algae, **anemones** (ah-NEM-ah-nees) and urchins, worms and sponges — not to mention all the different fishes — find homes there, too.

The plants of the reef, such as the sea grasses, are a crucial part of this community because they convert sunlight into a basic food supply by the process of **photosynthesis** (foe-toe-SIN-tha-sis). They also help to put dissolved oxygen into the water, something the fish and other animals need just as much as we land animals do.

The members of the community are helped by the presence of another element that most divers rarely think of as they explore the reef: nitrogen (NIGH-tro-gen). Nitrogen compounds are very important to the entire food web. They are produced by two types of organisms:

bacteria and a type of plant called blue-green algae. The bacteria and many of the blue-green algae are microscopic in size; other blue-green algae are in the category of what we often call seaweed, very visible to divers exploring the reef.

Many inhabitants of the reef community eat the blue-green algae, the plants, and the phytoplanktons. The coral polyps, however, are primarily **carnivores**. They eat the zooplanktons and other tiny floating or slow-swimming animals that drift within reach of their fingerlike tentacles, just as their close relatives, the anemones, do. The tentacles are covered with a stinging substance that paralyzes the prey when touched. The corals and anemones then pull the food down into their stomachs to digest.

Most corals eat at night. Many other predators are also awake and looking for food along the reef after the sunlight disappears. Shrimp feed at night, sometimes picking **parasites** off large fish. Moray and other eels hunt in the dark hours, too, often tracking down their prey by smell. Sea urchins and many mollusks, along with soldierfish, bigeye fish,

◄ A BARRIER REEF OFF THE COAST OF ST. CROIX IN THE CARIBBEAN AS SEEN FROM THE AIR

(INSET) CORAL POLYPS WITH THEIR TENTACLES OUT

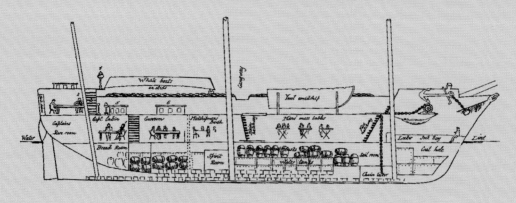

Aboard the *Beagle*

STAGHORN
CORAL

GASTROPOD WITH
ITS SHELL

TRILOBITE

The great nineteenth-century scientist **Charles Darwin** was the first European to study coral reefs. In 1831 the twenty-two-year-old Darwin began a cruise aboard the sailing ship *Beagle* as the ship's official **naturalist**. For five years the *Beagle* sailed around the world, spending much of that time in the South Pacific Ocean where Darwin first saw coral reefs at the island of Tahiti. He was astonished and intrigued by the life they supported and spent much of his time studying how reefs were formed. His investigations became very important to the work of other scientists, especially **geologists,** who were trying to figure out how landforms changed over time. He eventually published a book about reefs called *The Structure and Distribution of Coral Reefs* in 1842.

A PORKFISH SWIMS BENEATH
THE BRANCHES OF A CORAL

squirrelfish, and scorpionfish, all feed at twilight or night-time in particular parts of the reef. Some fish, such as barracuda, sharks, and some types of bass, patrol very large areas of marine territory, moving around from one reef to another.

During the day, the peak of the reef community's activity is when high tide and bright sunlight coincide. Fish that root around on the floor of the lagoons, such as the tuskfish, are very active at this time of day. So are the smaller goatfish that follow the larger fish, cleaning up the small morsels which the tuskfish leave behind. Butterflyfish and surgeonfish are herbivores. They scrape algae off the corals' outer skeletons, 'grazing' over the reef for most of the day. A few corals, such as the velvety *Goniopora*,* eat during the day.

Green sea turtles also live around coral reefs. Many nest along the Great Barrier Reef and in the Caribbean and the Gulf of Mexico. Loggerhead and hawksbill turtles also lay their eggs on the reef flats of the Great Barrier Reef. All female sea turtles return to the same beach or flat where they were hatched to lay their own eggs, a fact of their life cycles very important to the preservation of sea turtles worldwide.

Although corals need a supply of nourishment, they cannot tolerate water that's too full of particles, whether nutritious or not, because their feeding systems can become easily clogged. They're also sensitive to temperature: reef-building corals can't colonize below 70° Fahrenheit. Depth is also important. Some coral will grow in water up to 250 feet deep, but reef-building corals won't grow below 150 feet. This is because their algae, the zooxanthellae, need sunlight to help the coral build their skeletons. And below 150 feet, the sunlight — if there is any — is too weak to be of use for photosynthesis.

A FOUR-EYE
BUTTERFLY FISH

Standard scientific names of all living organisms are written in Latin and are usually printed in italic (slanting) type.

Hunters in the Dark

The largest predator of many reef communities is the shark. Among the reefs of the Caribbean Sea and Florida, there are about 9 common species of sharks, ranging from the dangerous hammerheads to the placid nurse sharks. Sharks' eyes are specially adapted to dim light, which makes them very good at hunting during twilight. In addition, pressure-sensitive pores on their skin allow them to detect movement in the water around them, even in the dark. So night-time divers visiting a reef would be seen and sensed by a nearby shark long before the divers would be aware of it.

SAND TIGER SHARK

Reef-building corals are called hard-bodied corals because of their hard outer skeletons. Soft-bodied corals (which have a flexible softer skeleton and were the earliest corals to appear on Earth) build only small colonies and do not contain the special zooxanthellae algae. Most of these types live in deeper water. Reefs often support both types of corals, the hard corals in the shallow, sunnier water and the soft corals in the deeper, darker water.

But even if the temperature, depth, and sunlight are right, other conditions might prevent a coral reef from forming. For example, the northern section of the Indian Ocean along the coast of northwestern India and southern Pakistan and the western section of the South China Sea are either too hot, too murky, or flushed with too much freshwater. The complete balance of temperature, sunlight, depth, clearness, and salt content must be just right for corals to grow.

Most corals grow very slowly, maybe less than two inches per year. The staghorn corals grow the fastest, up to 4 inches per year in good conditions. The outer, seaward slopes of a reef are where corals usually grow most abundantly. This is where the ocean waves provide both the most nourishment and the most effective cleaning system. On the lagoon side of a reef, the water is much calmer and the floating particles tend to settle and accumulate more thickly on the seafloor, slowing or preventing the growth of the polyps.

WHITSUNDAY ATOLL AND ITS LAGOON, SKETCHED BY CHARLES DARWIN

The ring-formed reef of the lagoon island is surmounted in the greater part of its length by linear islets. On the northern or leeward side there is an opening through which vessels can pass to the anchorage within. On entering, the scene was very curious and rather pretty; its beauty, however, entirely depended on the brilliancy of the surrounding colors. The shallow, clear, and still water of the lagoon, resting in its greater part on white sand, is, when illumined by a vertical sun, of the most vivid green. This brilliant expanse, several miles in width, is on all sides divided, either by a line of snow-white breakers from the dark heaving waters of the ocean, or from the blue vault of heaven by the strips of land crowned by the level tops of the coconut trees. As a white cloud here and there affords a pleasing contrast with the azure sky, so in the lagoon bands of living coral darken the emerald-green water.

Charles Darwin, Journal of Researches into the Natural History and Geology of the Countries Visited During the Voyage Round the World of H.M.S. Beagle under the Command of Captain Fitzroy, *R.N.*

AT HOME IN THE TROPICS

When you look at the map showing the location of the world's coral reefs, you can't help but notice that they are all fairly near the Equator. Only a very small percentage of coral reefs lie above the Tropic of Cancer (23.5° north latitude) or below the Tropic of Capricorn (23.5° south latitude). This is not surprising since corals need warm water in which to live. You might also notice that coral reefs appear near landmasses, whether up near continents or around islands in the Pacific Ocean and Caribbean Sea. This, too, is not surprising since corals can only grow in fairly shallow water, usually on the **continental shelves** that reach out from the shore before the continents drop off into the really deep ocean water.

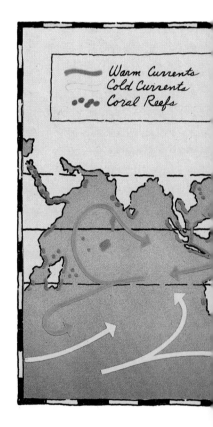

An Ocean in Motion

Ocean currents are created by a combination of the rotation of the planet on its axis, the barriers created by the continents, wind patterns, temperature, and the Coriolis Effect. The Coriolis Effect is a physical force that makes objects north of the Equator veer to the right (clockwise) and those south of the Equator veer to the left (counterclockwise). The movements of currents can get pretty complicated. For example, cold water is denser than warm water. And the deeper the water, the colder it is. Also, the saltier the water, the denser it is. So seawater becomes separated into layers of different temperatures and

Yet there is another, less obvious characteristic of these coral reefs: most coral kingdoms lie within the paths of what are called western boundary currents. A western boundary current is one that flows away from the Equator towards either the North or the South Pole along the western side of the ocean. These currents are generally warm because they are continuations of the main currents that have been moving across the middle of the ocean and so have picked up the warmth of the tropical sun.

The eastern boundary currents, which flow towards the Equator on the eastern sides of the seas and oceans, are too cold to support coral reefs. They have picked up huge quantities of cold water encircling the Arctic or Antarctica. Strangely enough, they also contain too much organic material—which is good for hungry fish and sea mammals but

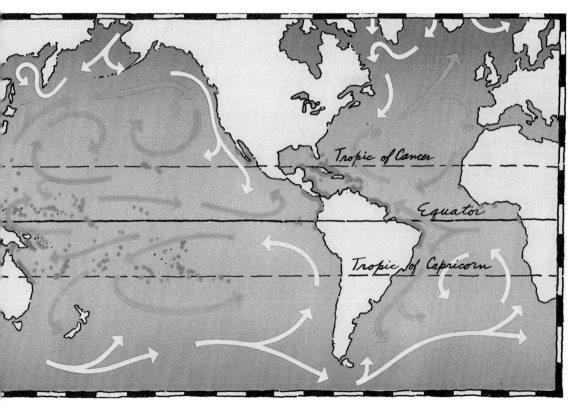

different **salinities** (levels of saltiness). These layers of water then move in different directions at different speeds. And each layer will have its own variety of inhabitants that are especially adapted to their own layer of water.

THE ANCIENT SUPER-
CONTINENT, PANGAEA

The fair breeze blew, the white foam flew,

The furrow followed free;

We were the first that ever burst

Into that silent sea!

All in a hot and copper sky,

The bloody Sun, at noon,

Right up above the mast did stand,

No bigger than the Moon.

Day after day, day after day,

We stuck, nor breath nor motion;

As idle as a painted ship

Upon a painted ocean.

Water, water, every where,

And all the boards did shrink;

Water, water, every where,

Nor any drop to drink.

Samuel Taylor Coleridge,
The Rime of the Ancient Mariner

'suffocates' coral polyps. Another problem is that these eastern boundary currents aren't salty enough. Put all these factors together and the support of coral life in those parts of the ocean is practically impossible.

At one time, more than 65 million years ago, Earth's ocean was filled with coral reefs and a huge variety of coral species. One of the few constancies in Earth's history has been change, and the ocean has been no exception.

OF CORALS, SEAS, AND DINOSAURS

ICHTHYOSAUR

Some three hundred million years ago an immense, warm tropical ocean surrounded the huge single supercontinent, which geologists have named **Pangaea** (pan-GEE-ah), meaning 'all Earth'. Although the poles were cold, the rest of Earth's climate was tropical and stayed that way for millions of years. Century after century, enormous coral reefs formed in the shallow seas around Pangaea with a profusion of corals, **mollusks** (such as snails, clams, and oysters), algae, sponges, **echinoderms** (eh-KINE-o-derms: spiny-skinned animals such as starfish, sea urchins, sea lilies, and sea cucumbers), and many others.

Then about two hundred and fifty million years ago, Pangaea began to break apart into two continents. As millions of years passed, those two still-large land-masses broke up into even more pieces and began to drift into the arrangement of the continents we know today.

Not surprisingly, all this movement of Earth's crust material had a tremendous impact on marine life. The land rose and

the shallow seas drained into the deepening ocean basins. As these changes occurred, the new continents began to block the once steady, regular flow of water that had circled the planet without interruption. Cold currents from the poles began to flow up under the tropical waters. Powerful new currents began to move in more complicated patterns.

These changes continued throughout the **Mesozoic Era**, the time period often called the Age of Dinosaurs. By the end of the Mesozoic Era 65 million years ago, the changes in the landmasses had caused major changes in the climate of the entire planet. Violent storms formed over the ocean waters, cold currents churned around the continents, and the temperatures of land and sea dropped dramatically. The average deep-water temperature which was 57°F in the **Cretaceous Period** (the last geologic time segment in the Mesozoic Era) dropped to the 37°F of today. Surface temperatures dropped from an average high of 75°F to the current 59°F average.

These catastrophic changes that geologists and **paleontologists** think may have caused the end of the dinosaurs also sealed the fate of the majority of Earth's

Nothing Stays the Same

Our oceans still grow steadily colder, partly due to the formation of the Antarctic ice cap about 15 to 20 million years ago. Also, as the continents have continued to drift apart, the seafloor has continued to spread and deepen. (At the same time, the level of the sea has been steadily rising. Since 1930, sea level has risen between 8 and 9 inches! Millennium by millennium the seasons have varied between ever-widening temperature extremes, and the tropical seas have shrunk.

Will the process eventually stop and reverse itself, with the oceans growing warmer again and the global climate once again turning mild? We don't know. But we do know that the drastic effects on the environment brought about by the relatively new human species are causing many changes in the entire global system. No one knows what these changes will bring.

corals. On land, although the entire population of dinosaurs disappeared, the mammals, many amphibians, and many other reptiles lived on. In the ocean, nearly one third of all families of living organisms became extinct.

It was a catastrophe for corals: two-thirds of all their species disappeared! Those millions of years of a tropical, unchanging environment had nurtured corals and the life upon which the corals depended for food without providing the

PLESIOSAUR

mechanisms to adapt to major environmental changes. They were 'summer' organisms suddenly faced with an unexpected 'winter'. Only a few of the thousands of coral species survived the change, those in the scattered areas of ocean keeping a habitat most like that in which they had first evolved. So that is where you will find them today: scattered outposts that remain from the dazzling empire of corals that once flourished in the huge, balmy cradle of life long ago.

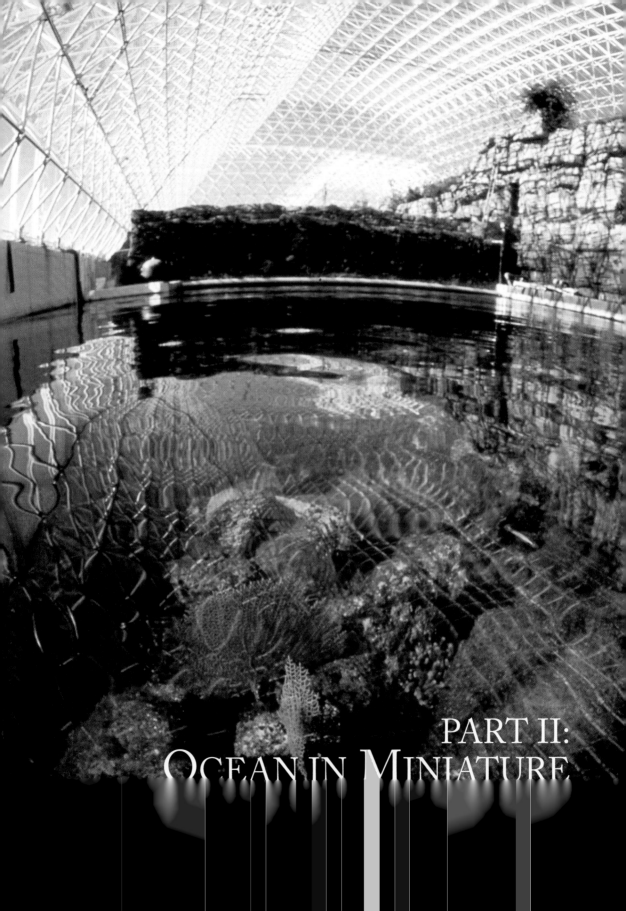

PART II:
OCEAN IN MINIATURE

HOW TO MAKE AN OCEAN

Scientists have been studying the ocean only since the middle of the nineteenth century; there is much about it they don't know. Such questions as, What is the role of the ocean in the whole global movement of carbon, one of life's main elements? Or of nitrogen or calcium carbonate? These are among the many fascinating puzzles which scientists have yet to fully understand. Without our ocean, we wouldn't have our life-supporting atmosphere. And without our nitrogen- and oxygen-based atmosphere, Earth would not support life as we know it.

The ocean is a crucial part of the puzzle of why there is life on Earth at all. Scientists in many fields are trying to discover and fit in the many missing

LOOKING DOWN AT THE BIOSPHERE 2

AN ARROW CRAB IN THE BIOSPHERE 2 OCEAN

OCEAN FROM THE RAINFOREST

Biosphere: The domain of life, the part of the Earth in which life exists or which can support life, made up of many complex ecosystems. It reaches from underground to way up in the atmosphere.

Biome: A distinct natural region where plants, animals, and other organisms live under similar conditions of climate, terrain, and altitude.

Biomes may be on land — such as rainforests or deserts — or in water — such as marshes or deep-water ocean.

Ecosystem: A community of living organisms and their physical environment that together form an inter-connected unit.

Biology: The study of life.

Ecology: The branch of biology that studies the relationships of living things with each other and with their environment.

Biomes: Key Pieces in Earth's System of Life

ARGALI MOUNTAIN SHEEP

There are many types of biomes on Earth, and their differences are not only whether they are on land or in water. Their positions in the climate zones have a lot to do with their major features of seasons and weather. As you move away from the Equator, the biomes change. Tropical biomes are much milder than temperate biomes because the sun is always overhead. But biomes farther from the Equator are angled away from the sun during half of the year and undergo the extremes of a winter season.

A second major shaper of a biome is its **altitude**, meaning how high above sea level a particular region is. Altitude (or elevation) also helps to determine seasons and weather. A tropical mountain area does not have the extremes in climate that a temperate alpine area does. Hence, like the bison of the temperate American prairies, animals such as the argali mountain sheep and the marmots of the high mountains of Central Asia are adapted to the extremes of their climate and terrain.

The grasslands in the temperate zones are similar but not identical to the grasslands in the tropical zones. The grassland inside Biosphere 2 is tropical, just like the other biomes inside the experiment, and is called a savannah. A grassland in the temperate zones of the North American continent is called a prairie. As you move even farther from the Equator into the arctic zones, the grasslands become tundras. Savannahs, prairies, and tundras all have different populations of animals and plants adapted to those special places.

MOUNTAIN MARMOT

pieces of this fascinating puzzle. It was just this sort of fascination with Earth's amazing (and, some scientists say, unlikely) bounty of life that prompted the creation of Biosphere 2 as an 'apparatus' in which to study how Earth works. This special apparatus offered researchers a way to bring together much of what we know of the crucial parts of our planet and replicate them in miniature.

That is why Biosphere 2 contains five wilderness zones that are models of a natural rainforest, savannah, desert, marsh, and ocean. They each contain communities of microscopic organisms, plants, and animals native to their area. And in each of their communities, the inhabitants grow, interact, and live out their lives under the watchful care of researchers (aided by an extensive computer system) who note everything about them.

Putting these communities together in a way that mimics the natural world as closely as possible was a tremendous challenge. Of all the wilderness areas, perhaps the ocean (what the builders of Biosphere 2 call the ocean biome) was the most challenging of all. How do you begin to create a replica of so huge a natural entity in a tiny space? How do you choose what is important to include and what is unimportant? What can be handled properly inside the glass structure and what would be too difficult or dangerous? The decisions to be made — very important decisions — were mind boggling!

The Voyage of the *Challenger*

THE CHALLENGER AT ST. PAUL'S ROCKS, THE ONLY PART OF THE MID-ATLANTIC RIDGE THAT SHOWS ABOVE THE SURFACE.

On December 21, 1872, a three-masted sailing ship (fitted with the latest steam engines to augment her power) sailed out of Portsmouth Harbor, England, to begin an adventure that would last three and a half years and cover 68,890 miles. She was the *Challenger* — loaned by the British Admiralty, supplied with all the best scientific equipment available, and manned not only by a crew of sailors, but most importantly by a staff of scientists headed by the eminent Scottish naturalist Charles Wyville Thomson. The first marine research ship in history was heading out to investigate "the conditions of the Deep Sea throughout all the Great Oceanic Basins."

From the day she left Portsmouth until she finally returned on May 24, 1876, this floating laboratory circumnavigated the globe. Her crew took **soundings** to measure the depth of the ocean floor, dredged the bottoms for samples of whatever they could find, tested temperatures at different depths, measured the speeds and sizes of currents, collected a multitude of new species from the waters, and **flora** and **fauna** wherever they touched land. And all of them — information and specimens alike — were analyzed and preserved in the ship's state-of-the-art laboratories below decks. The

JAPETELLA CEPHALOPOD

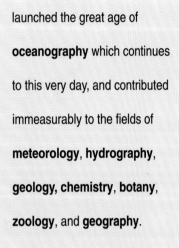

240 men and their ship endured gales, snowstorms, icebergs, meetings with cannibals, yellow fever, and drownings. Seven died during the trip and some crew members jumped ship in Australia.

Those who returned brought back the most complete, detailed, and voluminous amount of scientific knowledge of the sea ever gathered by one investigation before or since. It took 50 volumes to publish the results of the voyage! The *Challenger* had discovered 4,417 new species of living things, proved that life existed at great depths, sounded their deepest point at 26,850 feet in the western Pacific (not far off from the deepest sounding of all time at 35,900 feet), recorded the first accurate magnetic readings, established the main arrangements of the oceanic basins and the first plots of currents and temperatures, launched the great age of **oceanography** which continues to this very day, and contributed immeasurably to the fields of **meteorology**, **hydrography**, **geology, chemistry, botany**, **zoology**, and **geography**.

The door to the Great Deep had been opened — the unfathomable had begun to be fathomed! It was the beginning of a greater voyage of exploration than anyone had expected, one that scientists and adventurers are still committed to with the same excitement and dedication today.

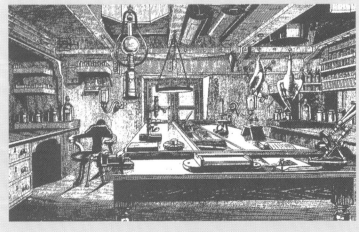

THE ZOOLOGICAL LABORATORY ABOARD THE CHALLENGER

AT THE
BOTTOM

Creating the Biosphere 2 ocean and coral reef was much more than building a giant aquarium. The Biosphere 2 planners hoped that it, too, would be an essentially self-sustaining and self-regulating system just like the other biomes. To do that it needed to be assisted in its operations by mechanical means. Since the Biosphere 2 ocean is so small, it must have mechanical equipment do the things that the rotation of the Earth, the Coriolis Effect, and the large atmospheric weather systems do for the Earth's complex hydrosphere in its natural state.

Because of the limitations of space and money, the Biosphere 2 ocean covers only 15% of the wilderness area — unlike the 70% coverage by the natural ocean. Yet even though our ocean is so vast, it has huge areas of what oceanographers call 'water deserts'. These areas hold only a small variety of lifeforms compared to the more active communities filled with many species living together, such as coral reefs. So in spite of its small size, the large number of different species gives the miniature ocean the same high productivity of life as the natural ocean has within its great distances and depths.

But first, before water or equipment or inhabitants were brought to the desert foothills of the Santa Catalina Mountains in Arizona, the foundation had to be laid. The depth of the finished ocean is about 25 feet; the foundation was dug deeper at about 30 feet. At the base of a hole measuring over 63 feet wide and 92 feet long on the east side of the Biosphere structure went several layers of material to seal off the ocean from the soil and rock below.

The first layer was a foot of concrete, followed by a special stainless steel liner. Ordinarily, nothing could be more harmful to Biosphere 2's ocean than corroding metals poisoning the water. Most stainless steel would do just that. So the planners had to find something different. Eventually they found a newly developed stainless steel, called 6XN, which releases metals much more slowly. To ensure the safety of the steel, a layer of epoxy paint went over the liner. Over that went another layer of concrete, sometimes 4 inches thick and as much as 12 inches thick in places.

The bottom of the entire ocean floor was covered with crushed limestone, just as limestone covers much of the floor of the natural ocean. In the deep section of Biosphere 2's ocean a layer of silica and bahama sand covers the stone. The basic form of the reef is made from 3,500 tons of limestone boulders sprinkled with a generous deposit of crushed clam parts, oyster shells, and reef rocks. In the lagoon section between the reef and the beach a layer of sediment imported from the Florida Everglades, along with its living cargo of sea grasses and tiny animal life, was laid over the limestone.

THE BIOSPHERE 2 OCEAN UNDER CONSTRUCTION

Essential Facts about Biosphere 2

Volume

Ocean Water:

approximately 1,000,000 gallons

Fresh Water:

approximately 200,000 gallons

Rainforest: 1,225,000 cubic feet

Desert: 778,000 cubic feet

Savannah/Ocean:

1,719,000 cubic feet

Agriculture: 1,336,000 cubic feet

Human Habitat (crew's quarters):

377,000 cubic feet

Air: 6,534,000 cubic feet

Area

Ocean: 7,000 square feet

Marsh: 4,000 square feet

Rainforest: 20,000 square feet

Desert: 15,000 square feet

Savannah: 20,500 square feet

Agriculture: 24,000 square feet

Habitat: 11,000 square feet

Lungs: 40,000 square feet

Temperature Extremes

Allowed *(Fahrenheit)* :

	High	Low
Ocean:	82	75
Rainforest:	95	55
Desert:	110	35
Savannah:	100	55
Agriculture:	90	55

AN EARLY FLOOR PLAN OF
BIOSPHERE 2

A COLLECTION SITE IN THE CARIBBEAN

The beach was made from bits of oyster and clam shells, sand from the Bahamas in the Caribbean, varying sizes of silica sand, and bits of coral skeletons. During the first year, the waves (made by a machine that rhythmically sucks up and releases water) continually eroded the beach and dragged the sand down into the lagoon. Over time the slope of the beach became less steep and the different sizes of sand began to mesh together into a cement-like substance.

The boulders and pieces of shells are covered with 'reef debris', a mish-mash of broken bits of dead coral brought from the Bahamas and the coast of the Yucatan Peninsula of Mexico. Living on these pieces of calcium carbonate were algae, microscopic lifeforms, and tiny invertebrates that formed the basis of life on which the other higher lifeforms would develop later.

All of this work with concrete and stainless steel and rocks and sands took months to plan and put together. But it was just the beginning, just the container for what was to come: water and life.

MORE
THAN A
GIANT
BATHTUB

WORKERS FINISH LAST SECTION OF SPACEFRAME OVER THE OCEAN

Creating a miniature ocean and reef was a goal easier to set than accomplish. Zoos and aquariums had built tanks for exhibit and laboratory specimens. But no one had ever created a totally closed ocean environment that mimicked a natural one in a complete, self-sustaining world, not to mention one at an elevation of 3,900 feet in a desert, some 200 miles from the nearest seashore, and over a thousand miles to the nearest coral reef!

It was a long and difficult process for Biosphere 2's marine specialist Abigail Alling and the other planners. Each step of the way became a set of problems to be solved before the next step could begin. The stainless steel liner was only one problem among many. Much more difficult to solve was the problem of pumps — one of the crucial mechanisms that keep Biosphere 2 alive.

Earth's ocean water is kept constantly moving by currents and tides all over the globe. The ocean in Biosphere 2 must also be kept moving to circulate nutrients, oxygen, and waste material. Constant movement of water is very important to the health of corals in particular.

So before the water could fill the huge tank in the ground, a reliable pumping system had to be installed. The pumps would have to move nearly one million gallons of water without harming either the visible marine life or the millions of microscopic lifeforms (the **microbiota**),

which are vital to the food web. One marine consultant believed that the chosen pumps should be replaced because they would slice or chop the small organisms. Luckily, the consultant was wrong and the pumps caused no damage.

The ocean water is a combination of Pacific Ocean water trucked in from off the coast of southern California, fresh well water from Arizona, and — strange as it may sound — a salt mix called "Instant Ocean" made for saltwater aquariums. Crews worked around the clock for several days to mix together this special 'recipe' and fill the huge tank. Getting the ocean's recipe just right actually took many months, since fresh batches of seawater with tiny micro-organisms had to be added periodically during the two years before closure.

Along with keeping the water continuously moving, the ocean also needs waste products removed. The first system tried was a series of troughs which contain mats of algae that absorb the waste particles. The water from the ocean is channeled into these troughs in a section of the basement right next to the ocean. Not only does the algae clean up the excess nutrients and wastes, but the cascading and splashing movement adds the needed oxygen to the water.

Even though there are sixty of these **'algae scrubbers'** usually working away all day and all night, the system didn't work as well as hoped. So just before the Biosphere was sealed, the planners installed a device called a **'protein skimmer'**. Later, the crew made more of them in the Biosphere 2 workshop. The

A ROW OF ALGAE SCRUBBERS IN THE BASEMENT

A PROTEIN SKIMMER

MARINE BIOLOGIST GAIE
ALLING SCOOPS LEAVES OUT
OF THE OCEAN WITH A NET.

protein skimmers are a system of submerged pipes that bring a flow of fine air bubbles up from the bottom and gather the excess nutrients in a foam on the surface. The foam is then skimmed off the surface into a waste bucket.

Another challenge the planners had to deal with before the structure was completed was contamination of the new ocean by construction dust and air pollution. The corals and other life forms were coming from an unpolluted Caribbean environment, untouched by the

Alkaline: having a pH factor of more than 7 (7 is the indicator of 'neutral' on the scale of whether a substance is alkaline or acidic.) Bones, limestone, and chalk are highly alkaline. When you taste them, they have that 'chalky' taste. If you eat too much of these, they'll plug up your system.

Acidic: having a pH factor of less than 7; having a relatively high concentration of hydrogen ions. That is what pH means, `potential for Hydrogen'. Lemons, coffee, and rotting leaves are examples of things that are highly acidic. Eat in small amounts only or they'll damage your stomach.

Everything is either acidic,

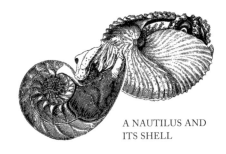

A NAUTILUS AND ITS SHELL

atmospheric debris of modern cities. Even though Tucson, Arizona, is considered a clean environment, it still has trucks and automobiles and light industry emitting various particles and toxins into its atmosphere.

In the winter of 1990-91, before the roof was finished, the new ocean was pelted with a sort of 'acid rain', which lowered the alkalinity of the ocean. The process ended up encouraging a rapid growth of algae. Once the roof was finished and the local rainwater was kept out, the ocean cleared up.

alkaline, or neutral because, in one way or another, everything in the entire world is connected to hydrogen — you, a raindrop, a rock, or the sun. Hydrogen is the most abundant element in the universe.

A RED HIND HIDES AMONG THE BRANCHES OF STAGHORN CORAL.

CORAL POLYPS FEEDING AT NIGHT

A REEF IN
THE DESERT

Earth's ocean contains many different
types of reef communities in many
different places. The builders of
Biosphere 2 had to decide which type of
community would be best to replicate in
their unique closed world. Because of
their proximity to the
American Southwest and
their northerly latitude, the
coral reefs of the Caribbean
Sea were chosen as the basic
model to follow. When the time
came to collect specimens to bring
to the Biosphere, these natural
habitats were to be the sources for
the new residents of the world's
largest man-made coral reef.

Even with the examples of these coral reefs to study and 'copy' and collect from, it was not an easy task to get living specimens to Arizona. Permission from the local governments had to be obtained before the crews even went out to collect. Then they had to get the proper diving, collecting, and transport equipment to the waiting ships — being sure to avoid the Caribbean's infamous hurricane season!

Hurricane season is a very serious threat in the Caribbean, as in other seas. One of the research ships the Biosphere 2 planners were counting on, the *Heraclitus*, was sunk in San Juan harbor, Puerto Rico, by Hurricane Hugo in the fall of 1989 along with hundreds of other ships! It took many weeks for the recovery team to retrieve submerged equipment, make underwater repairs, raise the ship, and then make more repairs.

The following year the research ship from the Smithsonian Institution in Washington, D.C., which was scheduled to take specimens to Florida, was run aground on a reef in the Bahamas. By then, the summer of 1990 was rapidly passing and the hurricane season was upon them. So collecting by ship in the Caribbean Sea was out of the question. The only option left to bring the right coral community to the Biosphere in time was to collect it from a place that could be reached by truck.

The best possibility was the eastern coast of Mexico bordering the tropical

NINETEENTH-CENTURY LIGHTHOUSES

Gulf of Mexico with its numerous coral reefs. After the many trials and tribulations of finding the right people to help and getting permission from the Mexican government, hundreds of specimens were collected at a site off the coast of Yucatan. Fortunately by then the *Heraclitus* was seaworthy again and able to help. Yet once the divers had carefully removed their specimens, lifted them to the surface, moved them to shore, and loaded them into waiting crates, the long trip to Arizona was another challenge to meet.

The first two expeditions for collecting the plants and the reef turf were fairly simple compared to the last expedition for collecting the corals and the larger vertebrates in March of 1991. It took four

THE *HERACLITUS* AT SUNSET

◄ A ROCK BEAUTY CRUISES A CARIBBEAN REEF IN SEARCH OF A MEAL.

days for three tractor-trailer trucks to make the trip safely from the Yucatan Peninsula to the Biosphere 2 site. Along with the crates of living specimens went artificial lights, temperature controls, pumps to keep the water circulating, and even some algae scrubbers!

As with many scientific endeavors, the expedition's success was due to the team effort of many people: Mexican officials, police officers, truck drivers, guides, divers, and collectors. The Biosphere 2 planners were particularly grateful to the Mexican government for its tremendous contribution to the project.

Many questions about what animals to include had already been answered before those final collections were made. In the first place, each winning candidate had to contribute something to the food web. This meant that they either had to be food for somebody else, such as the algae, or help eat certain things to keep the system going, such as the shrimp. But they couldn't eat too much or they would disrupt the system. So no tuna or halibut, let alone sharks or barracuda — they're all too big and eat too much, even if not dangerous! All candidates also had to be fairly hardy and easy to care for — no species that would go belly up at the slightest rise or fall in temperature or other minor changes in the water.

Eventually there were 41 species of fish brought to the Biosphere. Among the several hundred individuals, there were 5 species of damselfish, 4 species of wrass (rhymes with brass), 4 species of parrotfish, a couple of butterflyfish, sergeant majors, blue tangs, a Clark's clownfish, porkfish, flamefish, and even a squirrelfish, among others.

At last the anchor was up, the sails were set, and off we glided. It was a short, cold Christmas; and as the short northern day merged into night, we found ourselves almost broad upon the wintry ocean, whose freezing spray cased us in ice, as in polished armor. The long rows of teeth on the bulwarks glistened in the moonlight; and like the white ivory tusks of some huge elephant, vast curving icicles depended from the bows.

So Herman Melville describes the whaling ship Pequod *setting out from Nantucket into the North Atlantic, in* Moby-Dick, or The Whale, *published in 1851, the masterpiece of men facing their greatest challenge and their greatest terror, the sea.*

A NINETEENTH-
CENTURY DIVER

BIOSPHERE 2 DIVERS COLLECT
SPECIMENS IN THE CARIBBEAN.

SEA TURTLES ARE BEAUTIFUL TO
WATCH BUT ARE TOO LARGE FOR THE
BIOSPHERE 2 OCEAN.

SLIPPER LOBSTER

SQUIRRELFISH

The parrotfish grew rapidly during the first two years; some even reached over 12 inches in length. Parrotfish are 'grazers' in the reef community. Their beak-like mouths scrape algae (and sometimes the coral polyps, too) off the corals. They also help make fresh sand in the process.

The squirrelfish are meat-eaters which had been brought in as natural predators to help maintain a healthy equilibrium of populations among the smaller fish. But they managed to eat all the baby fish, the **fry**, of the reproducing damselfish, blue chromis, and others. Abigail Alling and the other researchers question if the Biosphere 2 reef is too small to support large carnivorous fish. They had known that the introduction of a species such as the aggressive barracuda was impossible; but are the 12-inch (and more) squirrelfish also too large to support in a closed system? More research about what makes a successful, self-sustaining food

web — both natural and man-made — will be an important part of the future experiments.

Meanwhile, **crustaceans** such as hermit crabs, yellow coral crabs, spiny spider crabs, spotted spiny lobsters, and slipper lobsters were also introduced into the experiment. There are also numerous mollusks: limpets, snails such as the West Indian top snail and the bleeding-tooth nerite (NEE-rite), clams and oysters such as the chione (KEE-on) clam and the Atlantic thorny oyster, boring and vase sponges, 6 species of urchins, 2 species of brittlestars, 3 species of hydroids, and 10 species of worms! Hundreds of species of algae and microorganisms are also very important because these are the foundation of the food web for everybody else.

When choosing the corals themselves, Abigail Alling wanted to be sure to get a good selection of different types, hard and

CHRISTMAS TREE WORMS

soft. Over 40 species of corals were introduced, several of each type. More than 500 hard coral colonies were included so there would be a large enough population to grow and reproduce. By the time the Biosphere was sealed in September of 1991, the ocean and its reef had a full community of hard and soft corals, **vertebrate** fish, and invertebrates, not to mention dozens of species of algae, **dinoflagellates**, and plants. The sea grasses of the lagoon would be especially important as a protective habitat for the baby fry, a nursery in which they could hide and grow unmolested.

During the first two years of operation, the reef lost some corals, particularly some large star corals, boulder corals, and yellow porous corals. One of the species went extinct. Some bleaching and algae overgrowth also occurred. But several species of coral have reproduced as well. Baby **planulae** (the reproducing forms of

coral) have been seen in the water, and the population counts of finger corals, star corals, and yellow porous corals show an increase. Still, the researchers of Biosphere 2 are cautious about making any definitive statements about the future of their reef community; their ocean is still in its infancy!

There were many differences between the 'natural' community as it had been in the Gulf of Mexico and the Biosphere community. The elevation changed from sea level to 3,900 feet above sea level, which meant differences in air pressure, in dissolved oxygen content, and in outside air temperatures. In addition, the coral community was no longer within the tropics. The site in southern Arizona is 32 degrees north latitude, at which the sun doesn't shine overhead continually

BIOSPHERE 2 DIVERS INTRODUCING SPECIMENS TO THEIR NEW HOME

53

throughout the year. The coral reef has had to adapt to a winter season when the sun moves far down into the southern sky and much weaker sunshine penetrates the mini-ocean's waters.

Man-made waves approximate the natural conditions but do not copy them exactly; for example, there are no storm or hurricane conditions inside the Biosphere! Nor are there migrations of diverse species through its waters, such as the migrations of squid or jellyfish or turtles or large predators. But this is all part of the wonderful mystery of the experiment itself — will a selection of parts of the natural habitat (hopefully the right parts) work? And what can we learn from it whether it does or it doesn't?

Certain conditions inside Biosphere 2 were created to be as much like the Gulf coast as possible. The climate of the entire Biosphere itself is a tropical one. Air temperatures are kept between a maximum high of about 95° to 100°F

(above the ocean in the rainforest biome) during the summer and a minimum low of about 55°F during winter nights (down in the desert biome). The water, however, is kept much warmer for the benefit of the coral community. In general it ranges from 76° to 80°. The tropical tradewinds of the Caribbean are mimicked by fans and pumps that keep up a steady breeze out of a tunnel on the west side of the ocean. Usually the wind measures a steady 10 knots, that keeps the palm trees and grasses on the beach swaying and rustling, just as they would in their original habitat.

A 'wave machine' keeps gentle waves breaking rhythmically on the beach. The 'machine' is actually a process in which vacuum pumps suck up about 3,500 gallons of water into a holding trough that runs the whole width of the ocean down on its southern side next to the marsh. After holding the water for about 11 seconds (or for however long the crew has programmed the system), the pumps suddenly release all the water in one huge whoosh! This creates the wave that moves across the entire length of the ocean until it rolls over the reef, then the lagoon, and onto the beach. It's not a crashing surf, but it does the job of keeping the water and its particles of nutrients, wastes, and sediments in healthy circulation.

THE BIOSPHERE 2 BEACH WITH
RAINFOREST TREES ABOVE

A DIVER PHOTOGRAPHS BIOSPHERE 2 REEF LIFE.

UNDER WATCHFUL EYES

Marine biologist Abigail Alling and fellow crewmember Mark Van Thillo (TEE-low) regularly don their wetsuits and dive underwater to monitor the condition of this unusual community. One of their most important research projects is to videotape individual corals regularly to keep track of their health over time. They also collect all kinds of other data, such as temperatures, salt content, light levels, amounts of carbon dioxide, variations in reproduction, etc., to compare the Biosphere 2 ecosystem with natural Caribbean coral ecosystems.

Scientists from other institutions participate in these projects, also. One study involves the regular comparison of the microbiotic lifeforms in Biosphere 2 with those of a site off the coast of Belize. Another part of this study involves the examination of an unexpected growth on the ocean rocks and window glass dubbed the 'grey slime'. Under the microscope, the grey slime revealed a species of algae called **chlorella** (klah-REL-ah) and

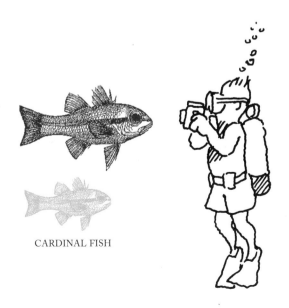

CARDINAL FISH

microcrustaceans called **tanaids** (tah-NAY-ids). These uninvited inhabitants of Biosphere 2 are now a favorite food of the French angelfish, who regularly try to chase the cardinalfish and grunts (yes, that's their real name) away from 'their' food.

One of the puzzles that Biosphere researchers hope to learn more about through their experiments and observations is, just how much can a coral reef system differ from normal conditions before it's in danger of dying? In other words, what extremes can a healthy coral reef tolerate?

Another interesting area of study is the connection of coral reefs with global cycles, such as the age-old movement of carbon through the Earth system. The tremendous biological activity of reef life in turn fuels intense **biogeochemical** activities in its surroundings. There is much in this area of oceanography, ocean chemistry, and marine biology that scientists are beginning to explore. The role of corals and their calcium carbonate skeletons in maintaining or moving carbon — the basis of all living cells — and the role of the ocean with respect to the global atmosphere are questions that Biosphere 2 might help to answer.

The builders of Biosphere 2 were very pleased that in spite of all the problems of creating a healthy ocean system, they were successful in reaching their goal. Yet it

GAIE ALLING CHECKS THE HEALTH OF CORALS.

does not succeed without ongoing maintenance. In addition to operating the protein skimmers to remove the excess nutrients, the crew must also frequently lower the acidity of the ocean water. High levels of carbon dioxide in the Biosphere's atmosphere

FIREWORM

stalking of fireworms, a reddish-orange marine worm that eats soft corals and anemones. Unfortunately, some of these pests came in as stowaways hidden in the reef rocks, reproduced, and quickly became a serious problem. For the first few months after the Biosphere was closed, Alling removed them. Even the tour guides would sometimes call the biospherians by radio to alert them to a fireworm spotted through the visitor's gallery window by the reef. Eventually, several hundred of them were eliminated from the system.

The fireworms weren't the only species that proved to be a problem. Two of the three lobster species, the Spanish and the striped lobsters, became especially good at harvesting the snails, which are important in controlling the growth of algae. Without the snails 'mowing the reef', the algae could smother the corals. So the offending lobsters were also eliminated from the system and became a delicious meal for the crew — another example of the humans acting out their role as **keystone predators** that keep other predatory species in check.

One of the species of marine life on the reef being watched as an indicator of the health of the community is the unusual giant clam. Open to the sun during the

diffuse into the ocean and lower the pH (raising the acidity), which isn't good for corals. So the crew must frequently add **bicarbonates** and **carbonates** to the water to keep it properly alkaline. The planners had anticipated the rise of carbon dioxide and had stockpiled 3,000 pounds of carbonates inside in advance.

Another task is keeping watch over the balance of species as the ocean and its reef evolve over time. A case in point is the day, tiny algae live on its huge 'lips' and photosynthesize, providing the clam with food and producing oxygen for the neighboring inhabitants as well. In a healthy ecosystem, the lips of the giant clam maintain brilliant colors of purple, blue, and green. So as long as the color of the giant clam in Biosphere 2 stays vibrant, all is probably well with the water in general. Originally there were two of these giant clam '**indicator species**', but unfortunately one species was eaten by a trigger fish and a stowaway octopus! The biospherians removed the octopus and trigger fish, and the remaining species, at last report, was doing fine.

Just as the coral reef inside Biosphere 2 is being watched and studied, so are coral reefs all over the world. One of the primary causes for concern is the destruction of reefs by people. Chemical and agricultural wastes are often allowed to wash out into the ocean along populated coasts, polluting the waters around coral reefs. Sometimes the flushing of heated waters from industrial manufacturing and nuclear power plants also destroys reefs. Dumping sewage and trash off our coasts also contributes to the problems facing our marine systems.

Oil slicks and oil spills are obviously just as dangerous to coral reefs as they are to any other marine ecosystem. Ships, sometimes even tourist boats, often run aground on reefs. Anchors can break off huge chunks of coral that took hundreds of years to form. Even pleasure divers often damage coral reefs unintentionally, not to mention poachers who remove corals and tropical fish to sell. Some people even intentionally destroy coral reefs to make way for construction projects and airport runways.

Humans, however, are not the only dangers. There are also natural predators of corals. Butterfly fish 'graze' on coral algae and corals by taking little bites of coral flesh. Some species of butterfly fish move from clump to clump in a fairly small territory, but other species may graze over an area as large as 100 square yards! Fireworms, some crabs, and some snails, such as the chocolate-lined top snail, also eat corals.

One of the most infamous threats to coral reefs is the crown-of-thorns starfish, which is a serious problem — especially along the Great Barrier Reef off the eastern coast of Australia. The crown-of-thorns settles onto a coral colony at night (when the coral polyps emerge from their cups), pushes out its stomach, and eats all the living polyps underneath it. When the sun comes up, the starfish leaves for a safe hiding place, leaving behind a bare white coral skeleton. Not only do these creeping vandals wreck havoc on the corals, but the other lifeforms that depend on the corals also die!

BOULDER CORAL

These predators and other dangers, such as people, are all being monitored and studied by scientists and environmentalists around the world. Their research is very important in determining what can and should be done to protect our remaining coral reef communities and to restore the ones already damaged. The researchers at Biosphere 2 also hope their work will contribute to the welfare of corals of the world as they learn more about coral reef communities and the communities' interactions with the ocean system as a whole.

A GIANT CLAM

A PARROTFISH

Abigail Alling and others at Biosphere 2 have helped set up the Planetary Coral Reef Foundation to study coral reefs and other marine life and to include its findings in a world-wide scientific network of coral and marshland studies. The foundation's headquarters are on the coast of the tiny

A SCHOOL OF GRUNTS

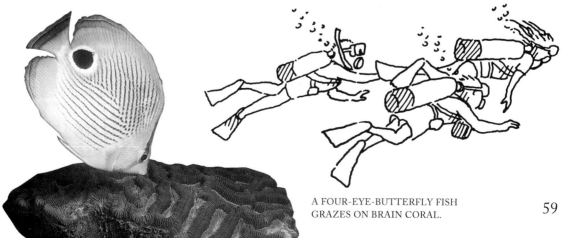

A FOUR-EYE-BUTTERFLY FISH
GRAZES ON BRAIN CORAL.

59

country of Belize in Central America. The foundation has begun long-term research on coral populations, microscopic organisms, and ocean chemistry. This organization and others like it, both private and public, are vitally concerned with the loss of reefs and what the loss of these often fragile marine ecosystems may indicate about the health of the whole oceanic system.

Coral research also fits into other intriguing scientific investigations in unusual ways. As mentioned before, the disappearance of the dinosaurs happened at the same time as a mass extinction of corals, which helps to support the theory that an asteroid or comet collision drastically changed Earth's environment at the end of the Cretaceous Period long ago. Another interesting finding from research on fossil corals involves the growth rings left behind on their skeletons, similar to the growth rings formed by trees. Paleontologists have discovered that these rings show that some 400 million years

ago the Earth year used to be 400 days long, not 365 days as it is today.

As marine biologists, paleontologists, microbiologists, oceanographers, and other scientists continue this fascinating research, who knows what wonders these remarkable underwater gardens will reveal. And the unique experiment of Biosphere 2 will probably be an important part of this research, bringing much new knowledge to light. We have so much to learn!

If those visitors from Outer Space include Earth in their vacation plans, perhaps the coral reefs will be a galaxy-famous 'must see'. But whether you're a scientist, a diver, or a curious tourist, most of us hope that the mysterious and magical world of coral reefs will always remain one of our most precious and cherished resources. May you be lucky and find yourself spellbound too someday.

Design by Kimura-Bingham Design. Illustrations by David Fischer.
Engravings from public archival sources.

PHOTOGRAPHS: Page 4, Tom Lamb. Page 5, D. P. Snyder. Page 7, Gonzalo Arcila. Page 8, courtesy of NASA. Page 11, courtesy of NASA. Page 12, top, courtesy of NASA; bottom, Gonzalo Arcila. Pages 18-19, courtesy of U.S. Navy. Pages 20-21, Gonzalo Arcila. Page 22, Walter Adey; inset, Gonzalo Arcila. Pages 24-25, Gonzalo Arcila. Page 26, Linnea Gentry. Page 33, Fernando Monasterio. Page 34, bottom, Gonzalo Arcila. Pages 34-35, C. Allan Morgan. Page 41, C. Allan Morgan. Page 43, top, Gonzalo Arcila; bottom, C. Allan Morgan. Pages 44-45, C. Allan Morgan. Page 45, left, Abigail Alling; right, Matt Finn. Page 46, Gill Kenny. Page 47, top & bottom, Gonzalo Arcila. Page 48, Gonzalo Arcila. Page 49, John Horniblow. Page 51, top & bottom, Gonzalo Arcila. Page 52, left & right, Gonzalo Arcila. Page 53, top, Walter Adey; bottom, Gill Kenny. Page 55, Gill Kenny. Pages 56-57, Gonzalo Arcila. Page 58-59, Gonzalo Arcila.

No part of this publication may be reproduced or transmitted in any form or by any means, electronic or mechanical, including photocopy, recording, or any information storage and retrieval system, without permission in writing from the publisher. The Biosphere Press and its logo are trademarks of Space Biospheres Ventures. Requests for permission to make copies of any part of the work should be mailed to: *Permissions, The Biosphere Press, P.O. Box 689, Oracle, AZ 85623 USA*

GLOSSARY

abyss: deep ocean waters, a bottomless gulf.

acidic: having a pH factor of less than 7; having a relatively high concentration of hydrogen ions.

algae: the simplest forms of green organisms, such as the green scum that forms on the sides of swimming pools.

algae scrubbers: a system in the Biosphere 2 ocean to eliminate waste products.

alkaline: having a pH factor of more than 7; having a relatively low concentration of hydrogen ions.

anemones: solitary flowerlike polyps related to corals.

aphotic: referring to deep ocean zones that do not receive sunlight.

atolls: reefs in the shape of a ring, surrounded by the ocean on their outside but encircling lagoons within.

axis: the imaginary line running through the Earth from pole to pole that the Earth rotates around.

bacteria: a large group of microscopic organisms with single-celled bodies, which live in water, soil, or in the bodies of plants and animals.

barrier reefs: long, narrow reefs separated from the land by an equally long channel of calm seawater.

benthic: the ocean floor.

bicarbonate: an acid containing the element carbon.

biogeochemical: referring to the interactions of biologic, geologic, and chemical activities in Earth's system.

biology: the science that studies all forms of life.

biome: a distinct natural region where plants, animals, and other organisms live under similar conditions of climate, terrain, and altitude.

biosphere: the domain of life, the part of Earth in which life exists or which can support life, made up of many complex ecosystems.

botany: the branch of biology that specializes in the study of plants.

calcium carbonate: a natural compound that is found in such things as bones, shells, and the outer parts of coral reefs.

calcium salt: a salt containing the element calcium.

carbonate: a salt containing the element carbon.

carnivores: animals, such as sharks and lions, whose diet consists mainly of meat.

chemistry: the science that studies substances and the changes that they go through.

chlorella: a type of single-celled algae.

coelacanth: an ancient fish that was believed extinct until live specimens were caught off the coast of Africa.

continental shelves: the shallow areas of the ocean around the major continents.

Cretaceous Period: the time period in Earth's history that began about 135 million years ago and ended about 70 million years ago.

crustaceans: marine animals, such as crabs and lobsters, with a hard external shell.

Charles Darwin: the nineteenth-century British scientist who developed the Theory of Evolution in his famous book, *The Origin of Species by Means of Natural Selection*.

dinoflagellates: a type of marine plankton.

echinoderms: spiny-skinned animals such as starfish and sea urchins.

ecology: the branch of biology that studies the relationships of living things.

ecosystem: a community of living organisms and their environment which together form a functioning unit.

equatorial belt: regions near the Equator; the tropics.

euphotic: the zone of ocean water that receives sunlight.

estuary: a marshy area where a river or stream joins a large saltwater lake or the ocean.

evaporation: the process by which liquid water changes into water vapor.

fauna: all the animals of a particular region.

flora: all the plants of a particular region.

food web: the complex cycle of food, food eaters, and waste matter.

fringing reefs: small reefs that are found in shallow waters near shore.

fry: recently hatched baby fish.

geography: the study of the surface of the Earth, especially the relationship between humans and the environment.

geology: the study of the history of the Earth as it is recorded in rocks.

hydrography: the study and charting of seas, lakes, and rivers.

hydrosphere: all the water on the surface of the Earth including water vapor and ice.

indicator species: a species that indicates the general health of an ecosystem.

invertebrates: any multi-celled animal lacking a backbone.

keystone predators: the most important animals in an ecosystem that prey on other animals and thus help to control their populations.

krill: tiny shrimplike animals that are the main food of many ocean creatures.

lagoon: an area of calm water encircled by a coral atoll.

Mesozoic Era: the time period in Earth's history that lasted from 230 million years ago until 65 million years ago. Also known as the Age of Reptiles.

meteorology: the science that studies the atmosphere and weather.

microbiota: microscopic plants and animals.

mollusks: soft-bodied marine animals, such as clams and oysters, that have a hard external shell.

naturalist: a scientist, such as a field biologist, who studies living things and their history.

neritic: the area of the ocean that is near the shore.

oceanography: the science that studies all aspects of the Earth's oceans.

paleontologist: a scientist who studies fossils to learn about Earth's past.

Pangaea: the giant landmass that existed on the Earth 200 million years ago which eventually separated into the continents we know today.

parasite: a plant or animal that lives off a living host without contributing anything to the host's survival.

pelagic: all the ocean water above the floor.

photosynthesis: the process by which plants use energy from the sun to make their food from water and carbon dioxide.

phytoplankton: floating microscopic plants.

planulae: the baby, larval forms of corals.

polyp: a small, round sea animal without a backbone that lives with others of its kind in a colony; the outer skeletons formed by coral polyps gradually form coral reefs.

protein skimmer: a system in the Biosphere 2 ocean used to eliminate waste products.

salinity: the amount of dissolved salts in water.

sounding: measuring water depth with a line.

species: a group of closely related living things that are able to breed with each other.

symbiosis: a relationship developed for the mutual benefit of two or more individuals.

tanaids: microscopic crustaceans.

taxonomy: the branch of science that names and describes living things and classifies them in groups.

terrestrial: anything found on land.

tides: the alternating rise and fall of sea level caused by the pull of the sun and moon.

tropics: the area flanking the Equator usually associated with year-round warm weather and high rainfall.

vertebrate: any multi-celled animal with a backbone.

zoology: the branch of biology that specializes in the study of animals.

zooplankton: floating microscopic animals.

zooxanthellae: tiny, one-celled plant algae that live inside coral polyps.

FOR FURTHER READING

Alderslade, P. N. et al. *Reader's Digest Book of the Great Barrier Reef.* Sydney: Reader's Digest, 1987.

Arnold, Caroline. *A Walk on the Great Barrier Reef.* Minneapolis: Carolrhoda Books, Inc., 1988.

Attenborough, David; Whitfield, Philip; Moore, Peter D.; & Cox, Barry. *The Atlas of the Living World.* Boston: Houghton Mifflin Company, 1989.

Ballard, Robert D. *Exploring the Titanic.* New York: Madison Press/Scholastic, Inc., 1989.

Cousteau, Jacques. *Pharoahs of the Sea.* The Danbury Press (Grolier), 1975.

Darwin, Charles. *Coral Reefs.* (Originally pubished in 1842.) Tucson: University of Arizona Press, 1986.

Gentry, Linnea, & Liptak, Karen. *The Glass Ark: The Story of Biosphere 2.* New York: Viking, 1991.

Idyll, C.P., ed. *Exploring the Ocean World: A History of Oceanography.* New York: Thomas Y. Crowell Company, 1969.

Kaplan, Eugene H. *A Field Guide to Corals of the Caribbean and Florida.* Boston: Houghton Mifflin Company, 1982.

Mangone, Gerard J. *Mangone's Concise Marine Almanac.* New York: Taylor & Francis, 1990.

Moore, J. Robert, et al. *Readings from Scientific American: Oceanography.* San Francisco: W.H. Freeman and Company, 1971.

Myers, Norman, ed. *GAIA: An Atlas of Planet Management.* Garden City, NY: Anchor Press, Doubleday & Co., Inc., 1984.

Roessler, Carl. *Coral Kingdoms.* New York: Harry N. Abrams, Inc., 1986.

Sheppard, Charles R. C. *A Natural History of the Coral Reef.* Poole, England: Blandford Press, 1983.

Steere, Susan, & Ring, Kathryn. *The Reef & the Wrasse.* Tucson: Harbinger House, Inc., 1988.

Weber, Michael, & Tinney, Richard. *A Nation of Oceans.* Washington, DC: Center for Environmental Education, Inc., 1986.

INDEX   *Page numbers in italic (slanted) type refer to pictures.*